Shuttlecock Time

Mark Simpson

Cover by Kara Simpson

Printed in the United States of America
First Printing, 2023
ISBN: 9798218295219

Praise for Shuttlecock Time

"The funny ones were okay, I guess. Well, some of them."

—

"I don't get it. Poetry isn't supposed to rhyme."

—

"Could have used pictures."

—

"Actually, a willow doesn't look anything like an oak."

—

"It grows on you once you realize there's no deeper meaning."

—

"Brilliant! The best thing I've ever read! Also, I forgot my password, can you come over and show me again? Love you, sweetie!"

Shuttlecock Time

A Glimpse of White
René and Me
Ode to an Inside Straight
Mothers and Fathers
Don't Look
Letdown
Solomon Had It Easy
The Life of a Minor Prophet in Heaven - Act I, Scene I
An Imperfect Project
Memory
It's Not Fair
Primary Season
Fooling Yourself
Envy Not the Angels
Just Worse
Complicated
Poetic Devices
Still Bitter
I Was Wrong
This Gadget
For Me
Shuttlecock Time
Telekiniece

Next Time
The Poet
The Goodness of God
Lamentations of an Atlanta Sports Fan (Before Everything Changed)
Agonistes
Hanging Around in Ephraim's Wood
In Charge
You'll See
King James
The Warrior
Baby It's Dark And Stormy Outside
We Both Know
Madness
Fifty-something
CXLI
That Thing
Athens, By Way of Auburn
The Life of a Minor Prophet in Heaven - Act I, Scene II
Thomas, and Me
Catsmind
Unknown
The End of the Day
Montecristo

A Glimpse of White

A memory, blurred by half ten thousand days,
preserved and altered by the same recalling.
An image once, now more of a sensation –
plans gone awry, emotions overtaken,
calls not returned, blood pressure on the rise,
rushed conversation, scurrying here and there,
a panicked look, a corner turned, and then –
A glimpse of white. A stopping of the breath.
I'd swear it only happened yesterday,
but press me on the details and I falter.
Where was I standing, what had I been doing?
Was I alone or talking with another?
Did I remark upon the sudden vision?
Try as I might, these things I cannot find.

René and Me

René Descartes, he claimed to think and be,
but all such metaphysic certainty
is not an option for the likes of me,
so many other choices do I see.

Ode to an Inside Straight

O Heav'nly Muse, my inspiration be!
Lift up my feeble hand and guide my pen.
Help me to speak of Probability
And justify the ways of Chance to men.

Five cards face down upon the *feutre vert* –
Whilst unreveal'd, all futures they contain.
To look's to yield delight, perhaps despair,
With but a single draw to hope for gain.

Tight to my vest, I splay them with a thumb –
An ace! Ho ho! A ten, a knave, off-suited,
Then seven, with a nine the last to come –
All hopes for simple clarity refuted.

O Inside Straight, thou Temptress, get thee hence!
Thou Siren, luring all into thy flame!
Draw to the ace, or fold – that's common sense.
To go for eight is sure a sucker's game.

Temptation, though, allureth for a reason,
And undeserved hope doth have its charm.
To play it safe is tantamount to treason,
Or so I tell myself, blind to the harm.

Thus casting off all measured calculation,
I call, and toss the ace into the pile,
Convinced, though with the flimsiest foundation,
That Fortune will reward me with her smile.

But Hazard's not impressed by reckless daring,
And Probability will have its way.
Chance disappeareth not with mere forswearing.
Man's hubris won't exempt him from its sway.

Mothers and Fathers

A summer's day, a cul-de-sac, a scene like many other –
a little girl must prove herself the equal of her brother.
It isn't going very well, she just can't get it right.
The seat's too high, she thinks, *my chin strap feels a bit too tight.*
She wobbles left, she wobbles right, she can't quite find her balance.
It seems perhaps this biking thing is not among her talents.
Then out of nowhere something clicks, it all falls into place,
she's riding like a pro, a look of wonder on her face.
She's going round in circles, like she's done this thing for years,
her parents looking on with pride, her mother fighting tears.
"I'm doing it!" she gasps, her eyes all lit up in amazement,
until a moment later when she crashes to the pavement.
Mom rushes to her side, aghast her baby might be hurting.
Dad laughs and checks to make sure that the video's still recording.

Don’t Look

Don’t look, don’t look, a sucker’s play,
there’s nothing it can tell you.
Long hours yet to while away,
to go where thoughts impel you.
Resign yourself to fuzziness
when comes the unwelcome sun.
This night will surely end, unless
the long sleep’s finally come.

Letdown

The lamest thing I ever saw, and after all that build-up.
We'd flocked to see the great event, the local park was filled up.
Dark lenses clutched in eager hands with much anticipation,
penumbras were on every lip, a joyous celebration.
And when the moment came, a hush descended on the crowd;
it got a little fuzzy, like the sun behind a cloud.
But then the strangest thing occurred, as nothing really happened.
The almost-twilight lingered there, the sun's force barely dampened.
When it was done, the crowd dispersed, with much dissatisfaction,
a halting sort of sheepish grin the commonest reaction.
The hype and the event itself could not be more discordant –
a mere degree of latitude turns out to be important.

Solomon Had It Easy

When Solomon (and in the Bible, too!)
compared his lover's breasts to two young deer,
she never thought, "That doesn't sound like you."
Alas, I couldn't pull that off, I fear.
If I described your beauty as a river,
you'd wonder if I had a rare disease,
for I'm not one such rubbish to deliver,
and you're not one to wobble at the knees.
What can a cynic say that won't ring hollow?
What poetry will not sound insincere?
I offer up the simple words that follow
(though I do like that line about the deer):
  Perhaps I'm no romantic troubadour,
  but my heart's yours, for now and ever more.

The Life of a Minor Prophet in Heaven
Act I, Scene I

Nahum, a minor prophet
Man, newly arrived in heaven
St. Peter

Nah.: Behold, a new arrival! Greetings, sir,
and welcome to your heavenly abode.
For certain, you must overflow with questions;
please let this humble servant be your guide.

Man: St. Peter, this is really quite—

Nah.: Nahum.

Man: Gesundheit. This is really quite an honor.

Nah.: (aside) Not this again. My name, sir, is Nahum,
and I am at your service—

Man: Oh, an angel!
How marvelous! Where do you hide your wings?

Nah.: No, no, I am a prophet—

Man: Ah, Isaiah.

Nah.: (aside) Lord help me. Not Isaiah, sir, Nahum.
You realize there's more than one of us?

Man: By Jove, now that you mention it, you're right.
You prophesied the coming of the Savior,
and lions laying down with lambs – great stuff!

Nah.: Er, no, again, you're thinking of Isaiah.
Fine fellow, but between us and the stones,
he didn't mean it quite the way you think.
In fact—

Man: How very interesting. Oh my,
just look at where the time has gone—

Nah.: (aside) The *time*?
Good sir, it isn't every Dick or Harry
who has a book of Scripture to himself!
I'm right there, between Micah and Habakkuk—

Man: Yes, yes, you should be very proud, old boy.
I really must—

Nah.: Oh multitude of whoredoms!
The Lord revengeth and is furious!
And I will make thy grave, for though art vile!

Pet.: Nahum, you're talking to yourself again.

An Imperfect Project

In days of old, or so I'm told, when violence ruled the land,
'twas absolute that all disputes were settled hand-to-hand.
The one left standing would command the obedience of the rest.
He'd proved his right in all men's sight and shown himself the best.
'Tis now my fate to litigate disputes for all my clients,
and we pretend the ultimate end is something more like science.
But I confess it's oft a mess, justice is not the object.
For all our pains pure right remains a most imperfect project.

Memory

Where does the past reside? Is it still there,
in cortex, cerebellum, amygdala,
just waiting for the right synapse to open,
the proper sequence of neurons to fire?
Or is it gone, replaced and overwritten
by each new recollection of itself?
Are memories remembered or created,
pale distillations of an earlier thought?

It's Not Fair

The why is not important, or the how, just what the who is,
or was, I guess, because what happens after what I do is,
the who that was is not the what that she had been before –
to wit, my spouse, a status that she lost across death's door.
Back to the point – it matters not how thoroughly I planned it,
because, though it may seem unfair and nobody should stand it,
it is a sad reality in this imperfect life,
the cops will just assume it was the husband offed his wife.
Okay, this time they might be right, that's really not the point –
why should it be a stereotype that sends me to the joint?

Primary Season

It’s Iowa in mid-July, he hopes that he can make it.
He doesn’t care for barbecue, but damned if he can’t fake it.
His tie is off, his sleeves rolled up, his smile is fixed in place.
He’ll suffer through Des Moines if it’ll keep him in the race.
“Remember, sir,” an intern whispers quickly in his ear,
“don’t use that line about how it’s the Buckeyes’ turn this year.”
He gives his speech, he shakes his hands, he poses with a cow,
then climbs back on his plane and wonders where he’s off to now.

Fooling Yourself

The only way to do it is in stages, which is fitting –
it took too long to grow to lose the whole thing in one sitting.
You started off like Hagrid or some cheesehead in Wisconsin,
then trimmed it up a bit so now you're Jeremiah Johnson.
Next step, you pare the sides away, you think you're Tony Stark,
or maybe Idris Elba, but it's more like Evil Spock.
Now shave the bottom part and leave the mustache by itself.
You gaze into the mirror, whisper "Magnum" to yourself.
Then last, you know it's wrong, it would be better if you missed it:
you've got to do the Hitler 'stache, you're powerless to resist it.
For God's sake, though, don't make it worse, fight off the strong temptation
to post the pic and find that you're an internet sensation.
And when, at last, the end has come, the last bit down the drain,
you know it won't be long before you start it all again.

Envy Not the Angels

Standing their watch through unending millennia,
struggling to hold the deceiver at bay,
comforting souls in distress without recompense,
ceaselessly toiling to push dark away.

Halfway to God, yet denied His perfection and
subject to all the temptations of man,
never rewarded except by the hope that it's
all in the service of His master plan.

Fallen mankind is redeemed by the Savior, a
grace not extended to angels above.
Cast into darkness for heeding the call of pride,
never one yet was restored to God's love.

Just Worse

I don't know why I did it, but I did and now it's done.
Of all the deeds I could have dared, why did I do that one?
The plan, the execution, every part of it was wrong.
Draw up a list of bright ideas, this one would not belong.
But like I said, I did it, what's it help me to be bitter?
I can't turn back the clock, a better option to consider.
The mess I've made I'm stuck with, for the better and the worse,
although I rather doubt the better in this universe.

Complicated

Is was will be yesterday
and will be was tomorrow,
and isn't now was won't be then
with wasn't soon to follow.
I'm always here no matter where
I am or where I'm going,
and when I move from here to there,
I end up here unknowing.
The whole thing puts my mind at sea –
perhaps the problem lies with me.

Poetic Devices

I really don't get these poetic devices.
To rhyme or to assonate? I'm indecisive.
Sometimes I alliterate, at least a little bit.
What is enjambment? I never can figure it
out, and it's too late to learn at my age.

Metaphors, similes, slant rhymes bedevil me –
they play the lion to my poor scared wildebeest.
Personification, it's so very daunting.
The sun sits in judgment and finds my words wanting –
like ice cream at noontime they melt on the page.

It's really hard to write iambic verse.
Dactyls are honestly almost impossible.
Trochees sound like pitter patter.
Spondees, good grief, who would want them?
I struggle with amphibrachs daily,
and I don't even know what an anapest is.

So by process of elimination
I guess it's

F
R
E
E
V
E
R
S
E

for me.

Still Bitter

Donald Trump stole Herschel Walker
back in nineteen eighty-three,
weeks before I stepped on campus –
worst timing in history.
Greatest football player ever,
lost to mammon and intrigue.
Blasted Gen'rals of New Jersey,
fake team in a faker league.
Sure, we made the Cotton Bowl
and crushed the Longhorns New Year's Day.
Still, the thing that irks me most
is never seeing Herschel play.

I Was Wrong

That poem I thought I'd never see?
'Twas sitting there in front of me.

I'd read it once, I'd read it twice,
and though the words were very nice,

in form I thought it quite a mess,
with not a hint of beauteousness.

Turns out the problem was the font –
Helvetica, that dilettante.

But just a few keystroke commands,
and presto change-o, Comic Sans!

Its beauty fairly leaps at me,
far lovelier than some old tree!

This Gadget

This gadget, this gizmo, this thingy,
is quite the rage up in Helsinki.
All the Finnish girls say,
if it's used the right way,
it'll fill up the sail in your dinghy.

For Me

A mile into my morning run
I saw, no I sensed, a stab of sun
from fallen leaves on the ground.
I paused, and pawed around, and found
a silver ring, not new,
begrimed, and on closer view,
there was something etched.
Then with my arm outstretched
to catch the light,
the angle just right,
the mud cleared,
two words appeared:
For You.
But for who?
Me?
Please be.

Shuttlecock Time

I cannot quite decide if it's Einsteinian or Newtonic,
the way a shuttlecock so quickly goes from supersonic
velocity to something more like immobility.
Is force opposing force, or is it relativity?
It's likely wind resistance, as Sir Isaac would've said,
but fantasies of time dilation linger in my head.

Telekiniece

I think that my niece has got telekinesis –
she gets this weird look and I start to see bookends
fly hither and yonder. It's something to ponder.
Or else she's a telepath, 'cause in the aftermath
I get this feeling my thoughts she is stealing.
One way or the other the whole thing's a bother.

Next Time

I’m walking through heather
in cold, windy weather
while dressed altogether
in clothes made of feather,
and questioning whether
next time to wear leather.

The Poet

I sit beneath this lonely willow tree
and know, somehow, its tears are shed for me.
That something still can weep helps calm my fears.
My own eyes have been dry so many years.

Uh oh, hold on a second, I misspoke –
It seems it's not a willow, but an oak.
I mean, they look a lot alike to me.
Who pays that much attention to a tree?

Good thing I googled it to double-check,
but now my metaphor is shot to heck.
(Yeah, yeah, it's not a metaphor, whatever.
You pedants think you're all so bloody clever.)

Hey, Siri, does an oak tree cry? Well crap.
I should've started with this nature app.
Let's see – blah blah, deciduous, skip that part,
but hey, what's this I read about a heart?

"The heartwood is the center of the tree."
That surely sounds poetical to me!
Now, where was I? Oh yeah, beneath the will—
er, oak tree just outside my windowsill.

A hundred lonely winters has it stood.
(Wait, do they live that long? They do? Oh good.)
Its heart, grown strong, lends strength to mine, grown cold –
Forget the weepy willow stuff, that's gold.

The Goodness of God

At night when I reflect
on God's awesome power
and abundant mercy
I give thanks
that water
is not sticky
like Coca-Cola

Lamentations of an Atlanta Sports Fan (Before Everything Changed)

Adversity breeds character, or so we're often told,
but twenty-eight years later, man, this **** is getting old.
It started back in ninety-one, with blasted Kirby Puckett,
with Lonnie getting deked and Morris going ten – ah, **** it.
"It surely must get better," you might think, but you'd be wrong.
Forget the law of averages, it's always the same song.
A six run lead in ninety-six? No problem, we can blow it.
Hey, Leyritz, would you like a hanging slider? Here, I'll throw it.
Up five against the 'Stros, and lose it in the eighteenth inning?
Why, sure, just tell us what we need to do to keep from winning.
Brooks Conrad making errors, pulling Kimbrel for Mike Dunn –
so many ways to lose a game, why limit it to one?
Chipper throwing balls away, an outfield infield fly,
with bottles and dark oaths alike descending from the sky.
And now, Good God! Ten runs across before we come to bat.
I thought I'd seen it all before, but never thought of *that.*
It isn't only baseball, either, no such luck for me.
I need a drink whenever I hear "twenty-eight to three."
And when the Dogs had Alabama up against the ropes,
some backup guy named Tua something-something crushed our hopes.
My sporting past, I thought, had steeled me for the very worst,
but there can be no doubt, this ****ing city's surely cursed.

Agonistes

Oh, fickle mind, so orderly and twisted,
a battle zone, unceasing civil war,
with notions half indulged and half resisted.

So many thoughts, when banished, yet persisted,
appearing just where they had been before.
Inconstant mind, so orderly and twisted.

Ideas, rejected, fail to stay blacklisted,
returning through some dark revolving door,
those urges half indulged and half resisted.

Internal conflict rages unassisted,
myself against myself, each keeping score.
Disputing mind, so orderly and twisted.

The warring parts so long have coexisted,
I hardly know the difference anymore,
which thoughts should be indulged and which resisted.

No matter how devoutly I've insisted,
I can't resolve the conflict at my core.
Oh, fickle mind, so orderly and twisted,
with notions half indulged and half resisted.

Hanging Around in Ephraim's Wood

I should have seen it coming at the time,
but other things were pressing on my mind.
Too late I realize I should have ducked,
and now I find I'm well and truly plucked.

In Charge

I know it's a no-hitter
but I'm not going to say it.
Or move.
You watching this? I text a friend.
I don't say what this is.
I wonder if I've said too much.
Pretty sure the announcer has,
and that chyron is bothering me.
My brain knows it's stupid
but I know otherwise,
and who's in charge around here?
I'd flunk a polygraph either way.

You'll See

Oh those fools are who-whoing, they do that a lot.
How I wish I could silence them with a garrote.
They who-who in the morning, and all through the day,
and then half of the night they're who-whoing away.
It's enough to make one's lower incisors clinch
and one's stomach to burgle and nostrils to squinch.
With their singing and dancing and merriment-making,
do they give a green fig for a heart that is breaking?
Has a one of them stopped by or asked me to tea?
No, of course not, they're oh-so superior to me.
All they see is a monster, not one of their kind –
to my deepest despair they are willfully blind.
Well I'll show them, I'll wipe that smug grin off their faces.
I will steal all the stockings from all the fireplaces,
and remove every present from under each tree –
that'll silence their infernal whoing, you'll see.

King James

A nobler wish there's never been
than "peace on earth, good will to men,"
that simple reassurance of
God's undiscriminating love.
Imagine then my fear and terror
to hear it called translation error.
I'm told His peace extends, at best,
to those on whom His favor rests.
Apparently the whole enigma
comes down to a missing *sigma.*
Speaking as an amateur,
I know which version I prefer,
but how is one to choose between
Egyptian texts and Byzantine?

The Warrior

There's never been a year like this, he thumbed into his phone,
then settled down to binge-watch Season 8 of Game of Thrones.
He ordered pizza, comfort food to ease his burdened mind,
and cursed his fate to be alive in such demanding times.
A thought went through his head of politicians' perfidy:
a perfect tweet, destroying them and their hypocrisy.
His good work done, he turned his mind once more to fire and ice,
escaping, for the moment, this cruel world and all its blights.

Baby It's Dark And Stormy Outside

It was a dark and stormy night.
Do I think she will? She might.

We Both Know

At times like these I find that questioning the *whys* and *wherefores*
is really quite beside the point – let's focus on the *therefores*.
What difference, after all, who brought about this situation?
Assigning fault won't speed up by a moment our salvation.
It happens to the best of us, these momentary lapses.
Who hasn't known embarrassment from misfiring synapses?
So let's get out of this, and promise not to play the game
of whether you or I, or you, is really most to blame.

Madness

A different kind of lion, this time around –
no roaring gales, no final parting snows.
Instead, a weak wind drifts through empty rows
where no fans sit, no champions will be crowned.
March howls for moments lost, and in dismay
that April holds no hope of Opening Day.

Fifty-something

Thirty years or thirty months or maybe Thursday morning.
If God permits, a little, but not overmuch, forewarning.
The only guarantee, that time is shorter than we thought,
and in the end, our plans and expectations count for naught.

CXLI

In faith I do not love thee with mine eyes,
the myriad imperfections they expose.
Thy bosom's droop, confess it, I despise,
that lumpen mass where one would seek a nose.
Thy bristly skin is not for the fainthearted;
my scars bear witness to the dangers there.
And scent, good God in Heav'n, don't get me started!
No tanner's shop doth so befoul the air.
Five senses, every one of them offended,
yet here I lie, thy wretched, bonded slave,
their plentiful objections untranscended,
salvation only hoped for in the grave.
  My path, let no one counsel its adoption,
  save for one reason: lack of better option.

That Thing

It could only happen to me or to you
because only we two do that thing that we do.
You know what I mean, and you know that it's true,
we've done it so many times all our lives through.
We do it alone and we do it together,
I seem to recall that we once used a feather,
but doing it in that particular weather
was quite a unique mistake altogether.

Athens, By Way of Auburn

It seems a different world; perhaps it is.
The summer gone, fall quarter starting soon.
A dented Maverick, three gears on the tree,
northeast up 29, an hour to go.
Slow down, Dacula's cops are somewhere watching.
Past Auburn, where you know the mayor's daughter
(the one who almost cost him the election,
but that's another story altogether).
Whoever thought to name a city Carl?
Before the question's formed it's come and gone.
Bear left past Winder, take the road to Bogart.
(Alas, not him; who knew there was another?)
You feel it when you see the Pepsi plant
(though hell would freeze before you'd ever drink it):
You're back, a straight shot down Atlanta Highway,
and everything is as it ought to be.
Nobody goes that way these days, of course,
not since they finished laying 316.
Not even me, I must confess, though sometimes
I tell myself I'll take that route again.

The Life of a Minor Prophet in Heaven
Act I, Scene II

Nahum, a minor prophet
Man, newly arrived in heaven
St. Peter

Nah.: (sighing) Another one, so soon? Well, duty calls.
Be slow to anger, as the Lord commands;
Remember you're a servant and a guide.
Good morning, sir, and welcome to—

Man: Nahum!

Nah.: Er, what?

Man: It cannot be! I must be dreaming!

Nah.: You know me, sir?

Man: Oh, pinch me! I'm in heaven!

Nah.: Why, yes, in fact, but—

Man: May I shake your hand?

Nah.: Well this is unexpected, I must say.
Am I to understand you know my book?

Man: Know it? Why, it's been my lifetime study!
Perhaps you may have read my dissertation,
Nahum: A Minor Prophet Deconstructed?

Nah.: Alas, I cannot say I've had the pleasure.
By "deconstructed"—

Man: Truly masterful,
how you disguise your meaning in the text.

Nah.: I what?

Man: It's all right there in Chapter 1,
the way you use the Ninevites—

Nah.: Foul harlots!

Man: —to symbolize man's struggle with despair.

Nah.: My friend, I fear you may have missed the point.
I wrote it all myself, you will recall.

Man: And, oh, the way you brilliantly deploy
the fickleness of God as a device
to skewer man for his hypocrisy.

Nah.: The fickleness of God! Now listen here—

Man: I love the way you use the "vision" trope—

Nah.: The trope! My eyes received it from the Lord!

Man: It's very clever, here, let me explain—

Nah.: Abominable filth! I am against thee!
Let all that look upon thee flee in terror!

Pet.: I see you're making friends again, Nahum.

Thomas, and Me

I take my cues from Thomas J.,
the neatest writer of his day,
who never met a phrase, or clause,
that couldn't use a comma's pause.
With them, he was so profligate,
it all seems rather random, yet,
if you but drill a little deeper,
each and every one's a keeper.
His letters, well, I shan't reproach
his half-Germanical approach,
which seems to yield this simple Rule:
important nouns get Majuscule.
So take your *Elements of Style*,
and toss it in the circle file;
upon its rules, I'll gladly trample,
following Thomas's example.

Catsmind

why look, it's that girl
the one who brings me my food
wonder who she is

Unknown

Some ninety years ago, a grieving widow,
a second wife, much younger than her husband,
completed his Certificate of Death,
and under "Name of Father" wrote two letters:

U.K.

I contemplate their meaning with disquiet,
as understanding pierces through the fog.
You had a name, a son who didn't know it,
or never thought it worth his while to mention.

I comb through census records, and I find
your son, his mother, but no trace of you.
Were you a husband, or a passing fancy?
Did you run off and never see your child?

Or were you simply absent when the taker
enumerated those he found at home?
Were you cut down at Bull Run or Antietam,
or did you live for years and die unmourned?

You lived a life as other men, and yet
a generation later, what remains?
The only evidence of your existence,
two meager letters, neither one your own.

The End of the Day

staring skyward
needles scratching neck
roots poking back
midges buzzing ears
SLAP!!
an itchy lumpy kind of serenity
pondering ponderosas
wondering why that one seems out of place
and what's for dinn—
OWWW!!!

A thousand pardons, sir, you must believe me,
I never meant to step upon your face.
If you'd just drop that stick, it would relieve me,
and maybe you could please step back a pace?

soul striding skyward
across a crimson carpet
spread by the dying sun
to match the one
on the forest floor
maybe fried chicken

Montecristo

Adrift upon a wisp of wind,
dispersing into fuzziness,
now gone – but for a moment there,
perfection, and tranquility.

About the Author

Mark Simpson lives in Peachtree City, Georgia, the golf cart capital of the world. In his day job, he is an attorney litigating *qui tam* cases under the False Claims Act (look it up, he had to), which allows him to tell friends and family, "I don't do that kind of law." A lifelong Atlanta Braves fan and a Georgia Bulldog since starting college in 1983 (Herschel Walker's senior year, and, well, you know), he is used to disappointment, and is having a hard time accepting recent changes in fortune.

About the Author

www.ingramcontent.com/pod-product-compliance
Lightning Source LLC
LaVergne TN
LVHW010507160826
845677LV00012B/2710
* 9 7 9 8 2 1 8 2 9 5 2 1 9 *